The Layman's Guide to Suicide

The Essential Handbook Guaranteed to Make Any Problem a Laughing Matter

Rob Cummings
Tod Weston

Paladin Press • Boulder, Colorado

Everyone has a bad day, week, month, or year now and then, but remember there's always a silver lining behind every cloud.

So cheer up!

This book is intended for entertainment only.

The authors, publisher, and distributors have no desire to fend off hefty, far-fetched lawsuits that in some way try to tie in this humorous book with any actual suicides. Therefore, by reading this book, the reader agrees not to hold the authors, Paladin Press, or the book's distributors responsible for any legal obligations as a result.

It's a joke, so don't do it!

READERS ARE STRONGLY URGED *NOT* TO TRY ANY OF THE TECHNIQUES PRESENTED HEREIN.

To: _____

From: _____

I'm Sure Things Will Work Out with Your

_____
(Recipient's predicament, problem, or dilemma)

But Just in Case . . .

The Layman's Guide to Suicide:
 The Essential Handbook Guaranteed to Make Any Problem a Laughing Matter
by Rob Cummings and Tod Weston

Copyright © 1995 Rob Cummings and Tod Weston

ISBN 0-87364-863-3
Printed in the United States of America

Published by Paladin Press, a division of
Paladin Enterprises, Inc., P.O. Box 1307,
Boulder, Colorado 80306, USA.
(303) 443-7250

Direct inquiries and/or orders to the above address.

All rights reserved. Except for use in a review, no
portion of this book may be reproduced in any form
without the express written permission of the publisher.

Neither the authors nor the publisher assumes
any responsibility for the use or misuse of
information contained in this book.

Contents

Introduction	1
Getting Started	2
What Are You Going For?	3
People and Things to Die For	4
Where Do You Go When You Go?	5
Etiquette	9
Fashion	14
Your Suicide Note	18
Your Epitaph	20
Will Power	21
Things You Should Have Done (But Didn't)	26
Your Eulogy	27
Techniques	29
Ratings Guide to Techniques	30
Quickies for the Poor	38
Making Your Arrangements	45
If You Fail . . .	49
The Obituary	50
Terminology	52
Taking Others with You	53
Parting Words to Live By	54

This Book Belonged To:

_____

Potentially your name (or name of recipient if this book was given as a gift)

Preface

This is the self-help book to end the need for all others.

Having a less-than-perfect day (or days)?

Have you said you're gonna kill yourself lately? Or thought about it? All too often, people rush into suicide without giving any thought to the arrangements they should have made.

Maybe your lover, husband, or wife left you; you lost your money (and/or your job); you blew the big deal; the bank foreclosed on your house; and/or your kids are worthless. Or maybe you've failed in some other aspect of your life. That's OK! Regardless of your predicament, this book is for you!

No matter what state you're in, you'll find this book absolutely indispensable in the event you are making your final plans. And, if nothing else, it will give you some more time to think about it!

Intentionally written in a simple, straightforward manner, this book enables even the most confused and distraught to follow along with ease. It's loaded with creative, contemporary, and trendsetting techniques as well as valuable tips and insights on what to wear, how to plan it, how to do it, how to let others know you did it, and how to let others know they are to blame.

Check this book out (before you do). It's a handy do-it-yourselfer's guide that will provide everything you need to know while it eliminates all the guesswork!

Keep your chin up, and good luck!

—The Authors

Introduction

Happiness is knowing your worries will soon be gone.

How do you know if you're a good candidate for suicide? For starters you've got this book in your hand right now. It's probably because you've been having a bad day or week or month or entire life. You may be frustrated, desperate, hopeless, pitiful, grief-stricken, heartbroken, timid, yellow, gutless, spineless, and/or miserable. And possibly you have come to the realization that you have no one to turn to and nowhere to turn. Bingo! Read on.

From what to wear to how to do it, this is the all-inclusive guide to doing it right (the first time). No need to reference other manuals, nor be talking to your friends . . . if you really are ready to check out, this literary work will stay with you from contemplation all the way through termination.

No matter how awful you think things may seem right now, keep in mind that they may get better and that you are reading about various definitive means to your own demise. Therefore, we not only suggest but strongly recommend full psychiatric evaluation and care, perhaps followed by incarceration in a state institution.

Also, please keep this book away from children and the mentally ill, and in the event you do go, the authors would appreciate it if you didn't bring this book along with you.

Getting Started

No doubt you're anxious to get started right away, but take your time and read carefully.

Please keep in mind that we are in no way advocating the taking of one's life. Things may not have been going great lately, but maybe they're not as bad as they seem. Hopefully ***The Layman's Guide to Suicide*** will convince you to make the most of your life; however, if you are "pre-disposed," you'll find this book invaluable! Either way, it's a good read.

By following the simple step-by-step instructions you'll avoid the pitfalls of having your arrangements handled (and probably botched) by needlessly grieving family members or inept civil servants, and rest in peace knowing that it all went just as you pre-planned.

No doubt you're anxious to get started right away. Please don't skim . . . read carefully and take notes! Plan it right the first time, and you'll avoid a second attempt and further embarrassment.

Now let's begin.

What Are You Going For?

Sure you're upset, and you have every right to be. But what are you upset about?

Most of you will already have a reason at this point (it might already be listed on the first page), but for those who don't, we've included just a few of the favorites.

Suicides without reason will be labeled "senseless," and, God forbid, you don't want to be in that category! Therefore, you need a reason, so be sure to pause now and choose one (or more) on the following page before moving on. And no it's not acceptable to circle them all, rush off to the bedroom, and pull the trigger! Be patient and take your time!

Curl up in a corner (if you're not already), relax, and circle all the reasons on the following page that best describe your situation. If you can't find a reason on the list, you can make one up and/or write in your own in the space provided.

People and Things to Die For:

Here are a few things that "just make you want to die."

(Please circle those that apply)

LOVERS
- Unfaithful
- Lousy
- Possessed
- Unavailable

PETS
- Unfaithful
- Disobedient
- Possessed

CHILDREN
- Worthless
- Possessed
- Illegitimate
- Screaming

BREAKDOWNS
- Societal
- Nervous
- Automobile

NO PROBLEMS
- NO life
- NO girlfriend
- NO boyfriend
- NO marketable skill
- NO hope
- NO AC
- NO TV
- NO IQ
- NO TP
- NO cash (general)
- NO cash (for rent)
- NO cash (for loan shark)
- NO cash (for drug dealer)
- NO breasts
- NO brain
- NO ambition

PHYSICAL PROBLEMS
- Cellulite
- Acne
- Boils
- Hangnails
- Hemorrhoids
- Warts
- Ingrown toenails
- Indigestion
- Diarrhea (in public)
- Broken nail(s)
- Gas (internal)
- Gas (external)
- Out of gas
- Pink eye
- Red eye
- Lip blisters
- Breasts too large
- Breasts too small
- Obesity
- Ugliness/homeliness
- Underweight
- Toe jam

MISCELLANEOUS
- Pressed meat products
- Tight shoes
- Toilet overflow
- Jail sentence (and the inmates like you)
- Jail sentence (and the inmates don't)
- Employment
- Unemployment
- Filthy public rest rooms
- BO
- VD
- ADD

IN-LAWS
- Visiting
- Moving in

BAD PROBLEMS
- Bad clams
- Bad dates

PHOBIAS & FEARS
- Acrophobia
- Claustrophobia
- Hydrophobia

SITUATIONS & CONDITIONS
- Marriage/divorce
- Blind date (is your sister)
- Alimony
- Child Support
- Bankruptcy
- Recession
- Depression
- Failed (exam)
- Failed (in life)
- Celibacy (involuntary)
- Traffic jam

VARIOUS COLLAPSES
- Financial
- Mental
- Physical
- Lungs (left or right)
- House or building
- Bridge level above you
- Dam (upstream)
- Stock market
- Highway

DEAD THINGS
- Stereo
- Pet
- Brain
- Sex organs

LOST THINGS
- Tan
- Mind
- Job
- Keys

YUCKY THINGS
- Spiders
- Snakes
- Vermin

LEAKY THINGS
- Pens
- Ceiling
- Diapers
- Faucet
- Tire
- Colostomy bag

OTHER

(write in your own)

Where Do You Go When You Go?

If we had the answer to this one, we would have charged a lot more for this book.

Before you take off, it's a good idea to think about where you may end up.

Christians believe you go to Heaven or Hell, Buddhists believe you are reincarnated, atheists believe you simply cease to exist, and Vinnie Cottello (friend) believes you go to a 24-hour nightclub where the girls don't wear underwear. Whatever your belief, the facts are (A) no one has reported back after being there, and (B) once you go, you're history.

Now you may be saying to yourself, "Hey, what if where I'm going is worse than where I was?" That's the dilemma. Let's review a few of the common theories.

Hell

We know one thing about Hell . . . there can't be phones or mailboxes since you never hear from anyone who's there. Unless they're having so much fun they don't care to keep in touch, which is doubtful. It's generally accepted that the place is hot. But is it hot and humid like Miami, or hot and dry like Palm Springs? Our own theory is that Hell is a place where the beer is warm and the steaks are never pink inside when you ask for medium rare. It's a place where broken fingernails are common and your shoes are always too tight. Some say you'll "burn in hell." Does that mean your skin will peel for eternity? It seems

The Layman's Guide to Suicide

that Hell is subject to interpretation. Who knows? Maybe Hell is an eternal repeat of your worst day, or being forced to watch endless "Three's Company" reruns.

Whatever it is . . . well, it's Hell, and it's eternal.

Here's what you might end up getting:

- Constant sinus headaches
- Devils (and other creepy stuff)
- Heat
- Cheap diner food and lousy service
- Psoriasis
- A lot of heat
- Relentless diarrhea
- Night sweats
- Overcrowded housing
- Eternal dry heaves
- Serious gas and heartburn
- Endless blind dates with your grandma
- Rashes (probably from the heat)
- Broken fingernails with hangnails
- Unclean rest rooms
- A lot of really, really hot, dry heat
- Day sweats
- Everything á la carte
- Bad hair days
- No sweets
- No free refills
- Yacking, pesky neighbors
- Severe lower back pain
- Nagging spouses
- Rude, inconsiderate people
- Hot dogs on a stick
- Tax on everything
- No more vacations
- A lot of people complaining
- Reincarnation after suicide

The Layman's Guide to Suicide

Heaven

Everyone seems to have a different concept of heaven, but we know it sure beats Hell. Heaven is said to be the place above the clouds where your favorite television show is always on and the meat loaf is cooked just right. The problem is, unless you've been real good, you ain't going! You can't buy tickets, and there are no direct flights. But the fact is, if you committed suicide, you won't end up there anyway.

Here is what you'll probably be missing:

- Totally great sex
- Ice cream and yogurt
- Healthy candy
- Toys
- Free cars for everyone
- Juicy hamburgers
- Unlimited credit cards
- Free day care
- Swimsuit contests
- Cloud life
- Flying angels
- Mellow harp music
- Smiling people
- Friends with boats
- Light
- Expensive jewelry
- Nightclubs
- Three-day cruises
- Hypoallergenic soap
- Toilet paper
- 200 channels of cable
- Concerts in the park
- Vacations to earth
- Lottery tickets
- MTV
- Halo
- Clean sheets
- Bibles
- Theme parties
- 24-hour convenience stores
- Free yellow pages ads
- Free directory assistance
- Healthy, green grass
- Drive throughs
- Free major medical
- Free dental
- Home VCR rentals
- Great food with free refills
- Free parking
- Free long distance
- Maid service
- Clean socks

Reincarnation

If reincarnation works and you actually do come back, bummer. Hang on to this book just in case. While some religions believe that you come back as a human being, others think you may come back as an inanimate object. Bad deal to think that you could spend your next life as a blood-sucking leech or a grain of sand in a litter box. Worse yet, what if you come back as one of the following?

- A slug
- An anchovy
- A boil
- A gnat
- A weasel
- A toad
- A squid
- A worm
- Married
- Unemployed
- An attorney
- A cockroach
- A snake
- A pre-op transsexual
- A leech
- A chihuahua
- An unpopular inmate
- Someone like your mother-in-law
- Your mother
- A politician
- A broke cross-dresser
- A popular inmate
- Liver
- An asshole
- Earwax
- Fungus
- Nasal drip
- A virus
- Bacteria
- A three-legged dog
- A cotton swab
- Sputum
- Yourself

Etiquette

There is much more to suicide than running out in the backyard and pulling the trigger.

Nothing is worse than an ill-planned, haphazard, last-minute suicide. Although you likely have little or no regard for those you are leaving behind (or for society in general), it is still a good rule of thumb to take care of certain details in advance. If you don't, you run the risk of having your wake, funeral, and burial handled (and probably botched) by needlessly grieving family members or inept civil servants who may even assign your body a number and leave it in the morgue for burial if and when you are identified.

Therefore it's wise to mind the Ps and Qs of proper suicide etiquette. Keep it clean. Keep it simple. Be sure to cover all the bases, don't be drab. And don't leave things to chance: PLAN AHEAD! Lack of planning will surely result in a less-than-perfect affair.

By taking a little time to handle all of your postmortem details in advance, and by minding the rules of proper suicide etiquette, you'll be sure to get what you want in the end and make an impression on everyone!

The Layman's Guide to Suicide

RULE ONE: *Make It a Lively Affair!*

Above all, don't be drab! Funerals aren't big attractions, so if you expect to get a good turnout, you'll have to make your affair one that your guests will talk about for years to come! (Note: Press releases are a real plus!)

RULE TWO: *Be Neat!*

Choose a method that will result in a tidy disposal of your remains. It's trés gauche to require others to have to scrape up your scattered body parts. The basic rule of thumb? If you won't fit neatly in a lawn cleanup bag, you didn't do it right.

RULE THREE: *Accommodate Your Guests' Schedules*

Most of your expected visitors are busy people with lives of their own (unless you take them with you), so schedule your services to coincide with their off time. Don't have services over the holidays and try to schedule viewing hours that don't conflict with prime time TV, football, or bowling league nights.

RULE FOUR: *Send Invitations*

Advance notice will provide guests the opportunity to ask employees for the mourning off. Notification for affairs such as yours have traditionally been by telephone or word of mouth, but since you know when and where, why not send invites? Aside from providing guests with the place and time, you can also request financial assistance to offset expenses, prompt recipients to call your answering machine or voice mail for directions, and even generate fun money for the services with your own 900 pay-per-call phone number.

The Layman's Guide to Suicide

You're Invited!
Rock'n'Roll Gala Wake and Funeral
Two live bands, door prizes, and jugglers!
August 21 AT 5:00 PM
American Legion Hall
(no cover)

Funeral Party!
...And you're invited!

Call 1-900-I-AM-DEAD for directions
and all the details plus your horoscope!

Only $2.95 per minute so call now!

Party Time!
What: Masquerade Ball (and Services)
Where: Lazy Acres on Route 6
When: Sunday May 12 from 4:00pm til dawn

A REAL DOWN-HOME COUNTRY FUNERAL
Yes Sirreeee! It's a country BBQ!
(since my method involved gas)
Hay rides for the kids!
Call my answering machine at
365-5867 for all the details.

CELEBRATE WITH ME
COME CELEBRATE MY PASSING THIS SUNDAY
FROM 2:00 PM TIL
FOOD · FUN · ENTERTAINMENT · PRIZES
ONLY $5.00 PER PERSON AT THE GATE.
SEE INSIDE FOR ALL THE EXCITING DETAILS!

WILD, WILD WAKE!
GUARANTEED TO BE THE
WAKE PARTY OF THE YEAR!
I PLANNED IT ALL MYSELF!
8:00 PM SHARP AT PRESTONS
DRESS FORMAL, BLACK TIE PREFERRED
RSVP

To save time and money, think about mailing off your invitation as a chain letter. Keep in mind that your wake and funeral may not be your guests' most exciting entertainment option, so make your invitations elegant and exciting, and be sure to mail them in plenty of time (but not too early).

Enclose RSVPs to plan your wake catering (meat or fish?), and preprint a box of thank-you notes for your next of kin to forward for

The Layman's Guide to Suicide

you. Also consider mailing a stack of self-addressed sympathy notes to yourself to make yourself appear more popular!

RULE FIVE: *Record a Phone Message*

Don't forget to change the message on your machine (or voice mail) before you go! In your message you can give friends and relatives directions to your wake and funeral, information about your plans, and, of course, the gory details on how you did it. You might even arrange for 900 pay-per-call service if short on funds.

> **Call 1-800-I-AM-DEAD for directions and all the details plus your horoscope!**

RULE SIX: *Shut Off the Utilities*

Before you go, did you remember to discontinue your newspaper service, let your pets out, shut off your gas (unless your method involves gas), cancel the lawn service, cancel the cable? Pay the phone bill a month in advance (to keep your answering machine on).

RULE SEVEN: *Be Prepared for Unexpected Guests*

Guests will drop in . . . friends, relatives, servicemen, neighbors, curiosity seekers, your landlord, and the authorities will all be combing through your dwelling so be sure to clean up around the house (not required if your method involves gas).

RULE EIGHT: *Let People Know Who You Were*

Bring along ID! So many people forget this necessary step, which is critical to receiving credit for your act. It's ludicrous to think that you could go through all this trouble and not even be

The Layman's Guide to Suicide

identified. Make sure the material you use for identity is capable of surviving your technique. No, your driver's license (and your wallet for that matter) probably won't be readable after a successful gas explosion. Dog tags are most often recommended.

RULE NINE: Send Out Your Legal Forms

If you really want to make an impressive and well-thought-out exit, for a finishing touch, fill out your own death certificate. The forms are fairly easy to get, and by doing it out yourself, you'll be assured that it was filled out properly.

Mail your death certificate to the coroner's office just before you go, but leave the time and date blank (just in case).

Fashion

Choosing what to wear for the occasion means you won't get caught dead looking tacky!

At this affair, all eyes will be on you, so dress to kill. Everyone knows you had time to plan your outfit so there's no excuse for tacky attire. Be sure to choose an outfit that works for you (and your technique).

Without exception, photos will always be taken, afterwards. Therefore, if you plan on impressing TV and newspaper reporters, you have to dress for the part(s). Bright, flashy colors will highlight your corpse on the nightly news plus they make it so much easier for paramedics to locate your body. Potentially millions of viewers will see your postmortem photos, so don't be caught dead looking less than your best. Why do you think so many corpses are shown covered?

On that subject, police and paramedics are people too, so try not to ruin their day—keep yourself reasonably together in your choice of clothing and select a quality garment that won't end up falling apart on you.

Tie Clothing In with Your Technique . . .

Technique and clothing are so interdependent. For example, dark colors are fabulous for stepping out in traffic, while red is the obvious choice if you plan on ending up covered in that color. If you expect to be discovered intact, then anything goes . . . you may even borrow a special outfit from a friend since you'll be able to return it! On the other hand, if your method involves severe body mutilation, something tight fitting (like a wet suit) is more appropriate. If you really want to make cleanup a snap, a body bag is correct, and, if your method involves gas, you needn't worry about clothes.

If you suspect that your technique may damage or permanently soil your ensemble (or if you don't expect your ensemble to make it through the affair at all) but you do expect to end up in one piece, and you are planning on an open casket, be sure to have fresh clothes cleaned, pressed, and delivered to your embalmer. Backless outfits are most traditional.

Accessorize, Accessorize, Accessorize!

Try to select accessories that marry form with function. The right accessories complete your ensemble and will really make the outfit work.

For instance, if you're going by electrocution, by all means cover yourself in fashionable (and functional) gold, silver, or copper chains and bracelets to coordinate with your metallic clothing. If by gas explosion, dog tags will stand out (and are the only sensible choice for identification). Going by train? For women, a small overnighter says travel all over it and works best (i.e., will be found with the rest of you) if securely wired to your arm. For men, a pocket watch is not only appropriate but will also keep you on time! If you'll be stepping out in traffic, try to avoid flashy jewelry that will be caught in the headlights, and if you'll be slashing your wrists, be sure to keep one arm free.

To liven up the scene, other novelty accessories might include yellow crime scene tape (available at police supply stores), chalk (to outline your body), and red paint (to add drama to the photos and to confound the rescue squad).

A Little Makeup Can Go a Long Way

Your choice of makeup has everything to do with the lighting conditions and the anticipated condition of your remains. In most cases, photos will be taken under floodlights or with flash, so for contrast use warm reds. (Blue tones tend to blend in with your skin color.) And don't just concentrate on your face, consider other exposed parts such as your arms, legs, and torso.

Dictating Guest Attire

You've now decided on your wardrobe, but what about your guests? You'll be amazed at how you can get guests to dress up, and it's so much more fun when you dictate the dress code!

Basic black is traditional (b-o-r-i-n-g), but why rule out black tie? Or cocktail party attire? Or period clothing?

Everyone likes to dress up, and if you dictate the dress code, you'll give them an excuse to step out and have a little fun.

Theme Parties Make Clothes Selection Easy!

With theme parties, the sky's the limit! The outfits can be outrageous and great fun for your guests to put together. Consider making your services a pajama party, island party, toga party, pimps and prostitutes, cowboys and Indians, masquerade, etc. Use your imagination!

If you drop enough money for the services, you can get the entire funeral home staff into the act. Some larger costume companies will even deliver the outfits right to your site so guests can get dressed there and don't have to go running around!

The Layman's Guide to Suicide

Need more ideas? OK, how about everyone in fireman hats . . . or hospital garb . . . or rescue uniforms . . . or dressed as hari krishnas?

No matter what you do, THINK FUN, be creative, and get everyone involved! You might even want to hire a photographer of your own (to recoup some of the costume costs by selling prints to guests) even though the press will likely be snapping away.

Your Suicide Note

*Show everyone you really can write
and don't forget to let others know they too
had a part in your big day.*

Your suicide note will be one of your last literary works! Open to public scrutiny, it will be read by everyone from family members to police investigators, and, if you do it right, it may even be carried in local papers! Hastily scratched, incoherent scribbling on the back of a grocery bag or old utility bill just won't do. Spelling and penmanship count! There's no excuse for a poorly written suicide note. Try to keep it simple and to the point. If you're poor at writing, or illiterate, consider prerecording on video or cassette.

Be sure to write for your anticipated audience.

If you're killing yourself for someone else (or a group), LET THEM KNOW by clearly spelling out their wrongdoing(s) and referring to them by name.

Leave your note in an area where it will be sure to be read such as the kitchen table, taped to the fridge, or on the back of the toilet. Or roll it up in the sugar bowl for a morning eye-opener.

In a real rush or can't write? Use the handy form on the facing page. Although brief, it will enable you to quickly place blame and help authorities locate your remains.

The Layman's Guide to Suicide

My Suicide Note™

(Check those boxes which apply and photocopy as needed).

You may have noticed by now that I have taken my life, but if not, you might try looking for the remains of my body at/in _____.

As the miserable soul and loser I have always been and will not continue to be, I do hereby say goodbye, ciao, arrivederci, and so long to…

(Check those which apply)

- ☐ Mom
- ☐ Dad
- ☐ Wife
- ☐ Husband
- ☐ Girlfriend
- ☐ Boyfriend
- ☐ Kids
- ☐ Neighbors
- ☐ Dog
- ☐ Fish
- ☐ Other Pets
- ☐ Other (fill in) _____

I blame my demise on…

(Check all which apply)

- ☐ Mom
- ☐ Dad
- ☐ Wife
- ☐ Husband
- ☐ Girlfriend
- ☐ Boyfriend
- ☐ Kids
- ☐ Neighbors
- ☐ Dog
- ☐ Cell Mate
- ☐ Attorney
- ☐ Other (fill in) _____

I did myself in because…

_____
(Write in reason here)

I didn't want it to end this way, however, I absolutely could not stand to remain on this planet for another minute. Hold my calls, I'm outta here!

_____
Sign Here

Your Epitaph

Leave a lasting impression long after guests have gone home by engraving your words in stone.

With the right message, your headstone will be talked about for years to come. Following are some memorable suggestions:

I TOLD YOU I WAS SICK
YOU SHOULD HAVE CALLED
SURPRISE! SURPRISE, I'M DEAD!
NO SOLICITORS
KEEP OFF THE GRASS
HAVE A NICE DAY
HI, MOM!
GOT A MATCH?
YO—I'M DOWN HERE
IT'S DARK DOWN HERE
IT'S COLD DOWN HERE
COULD YOU TURN UP THE HEAT?
I CAN'T BREATHE!
WHO'S GOT THE BUG SPRAY?
DON'T CALL ME CHICKEN!
DON'T CALL ME LOSER!
TRY TO GET MY MONEY NOW!
THANKS FOR THE MEMORIES
DO NOT DISTURB!
I WAS DARED
I'M HERE!
WHAT'S THAT SMELL?
AM I DIVORCED NOW?
DO I DETECT RADON GAS?
BET YOU NEVER THOUGHT I'D DO IT!

PLEASE CURB YOUR PETS
911 WAS A LITTLE LATE
THIS ISN'T THE CASKET I ORDERED!
THANKS DEAR!
FORWARD MY MAIL TO . . .
I DIDN'T EVEN FEEL IT
RETURN MAIL TO SENDER
VANDALS WILL BE PROSECUTED
DO YOU KNOW WHERE YOUR CHILD IS NOW?
THE BUCK STOPS HERE
MY CELLULAR PHONE # IS ____
IF I ONLY HAD A BRAIN
NO MORE PHONE CALLS PLEASE
SEE YA!
THANKS FOR NOTHING
I'VE MOVED, HAVE FUN WITH MY STUFF
NO DIGGING
I ONLY WISH I'D DONE IT SOONER
NO BIG DEAL
NO NEED TO WORRY ABOUT ME
THANKS FOR THE GREAT PARTY!
GO AWAY!
I HATE THESE WORMS!
IS MY CREDIT OK NOW?
YOU'RE STANDING ON ME!

Will Power

A clearly written, properly executed will can provide you with plenty of last-minute snickers and cause family and friends months of grief in probate court.

"Will power" gives you the power to control friends, relatives, and others. Even if you didn't have any before, you do now!

The purpose of a will is to guarantee that your loved ones will get just what they deserve, and that's where the fun begins. Now it's your turn to have the last word.

Let's say, for example, that you're a homeowner and you're killing yourself for your next-door neighbors. Want the last laugh? Donate your land to the city for landfill, toxic waste disposal, an amusement park, low-income housing, or even a Chinese restaurant. That should drive their property values right into the ground! And it would be fun, right? But don't stop here, will power and imagination make a powerful combination!

We can't possibly cover every situation (since so much depends on your particular goals), but to get you thinking in the right direction, here are a few more . . .

How about bequeathing only half of a whole? A single breast implant, a motorless motor yacht, the key to a safe deposit box in an unfriendly foreign country. Got the idea now?

How about willing items that you never owned? The "hidden fortune" routine can be hysterical, cause great fights amongst those you left behind, and drive the probate courts crazy. You

Last Will & Testament

I, _____, upon leaving the face of this hostile planet they call Earth, do hereby bequeath and devise my worldly possessions* to my beloved (and not so beloved) survivors as follows:

To: _____ My: _____
To: _____ My: _____
To: _____ My: _____
To: _____ My: _____
To: _____ My: _____
To: _____ My: _____

*Items with asterisks to be shipped Airfreight, C.O.D., Freight Collect

I further request that the remains of my body be vacuum-sealed and forwarded via US Mail for eternity by chain letter.

In addition, I stipulate that, in order for those listed above to receive the inheritance I have entitled them to, they must...

_____
_____STIPULATION_____
_____
_____

_____   _____
DATE   DECEASED

- - - - - - - - CLIP AND SAVE - - - - - - - -

If you're in a rush you may use this form but please consult with your attorney.
(This form may not be valid no matter what state you're in)

might even print up some bogus deeds, bury some costume jewelry, etc. And since you won't be around to tell people where your will is, consider leaving a series of clues in remote locations . . . like on different continents. It's fun to think that those you hate will expend all of their funds traipsing around the globe, only to find you gave every last penny to charity.

The point is that your latest escapade will put you right in the driver's seat, so take advantage of it!

Will Power Is Incredible

You'll be amazed at the crazy things your relatives and friends will do to get their hands on your hard-earned bucks and belongings, so also consider how entertaining certain stipulations in the will can be. Creative stipulations will provide those you left behind with lasting memories while sending you chuckling all the way to the grave! Use your will power!

A Checklist of Potential Personal Belongings to Bequeath in the Will

- Accident vehicle
- Accident clothing
- Accident photos
- Back brace
- Bad pets
- Bad recipes
- Bed pan
- Black book
- Body bag
- Burial costs
- Catheter
- Club memberships
- Condoms
- Coroner's report
- Costume jewelry
- Counterfeit money
- Curling iron
- Death bed
- Death certificate
- Dentures
- Drug paraphernalia
- Ex-lovers
- Exercise bicycle
- Fake IDs
- Fine washables
- Food stamps
- Friends
- Girlie/boyie magazines
- Grocery bags
- Hospital bed
- Hospital tag
- Household items
- Illegitimate kids
- Implants
- Leftovers in fridge
- Loan payment book
- Lunch meat
- Lover
- Movie passes
- Organs or remains
- Outstanding debts
- Padded bras
- Penny collection
- Phone bills
- Press-on nails
- Prosthesis
- Spouse(s)
- Supermarket coupons
- Toilet paper
- Toothbrush
- Vacuum bags
- Wig/toupé
- X-rated videos

A Checklist of Potential Stipulations to Spice Up the Will

In order to inherit my fortune, you must . . .

- Shellac my body and leave it on display by the barbecue.
- Dig up my grave and sleep with me overnight on our anniversary.
- Have lunch with my mother-in-law.
- Have your right arm amputated above the elbow.
- Frame and display my police photo (30 x 40) above your fireplace.
- Get a job.

The Layman's Guide to Suicide

In order to be eligible, my body must be . . .

- Moved only with meat hooks.
- Kept on view in the kitchen of the inheritor for eternity.
- Buried under the family room.
- Driven to the cemetery on a motorcycle with side car.
- Kept on display with a daily wardrobe change requirement.
- Slept with once monthly.
- In attendance each New Year's Eve.
- Made available for carnival shows.
- Kept in a refrigerated unit in the playroom.
- Kept in the attic.
- Mounted (like a swordfish).
- Mummified.
- Propped up in a patio chair.
- Lightly breaded and sauteed.
- Tarred and feathered.

Where to Leave Your Will & Suicide Note

- Behind a banner plane
- Under your windshield wiper
- In a condom packet
- On videotape
- In the glove box
- By fax or telex
- In your lover's purse or wallet
- Microfiched to a contact lens
- Wrapped as a gift (perfect for the holidays!)
- Next to the body (boring)
- On radio or TV commercials
- In display ads in the newspaper
- In the oven (unless your method involves gas)
- In an Easter egg
- As a prize in a box of cereal
- On your own web page (Internet)
- On the night stand
- At the bottom of the pool
- In your stomach
- Spray-painted on your lover's car
- In your underwear
- In your bosses' e-mail
- In your attorney's court documents

The Layman's Guide to Suicide

Things That You Should Have Done...
(But didn't.)

1
Cleaned up your desk
2
Flushed your toilet
3
Left your car windows open
(unless your method involved asphyxiation)
4
Made something of yourself
5
Left your lights on
6
Solved your problems
7
Set your alarm clock
8
Triggered your car alarm (to annoy the neighbors)
9
Called the Suicide Hotline
10
Ordered your casket
11
Broken your date for the evening of
12
Ordered take-out just before
13
Seen a psychiatrist

Your Eulogy

Since you know yourself better than anyone on the guest list, why not prerecord your own?

With videotape you can "appear live" right where the action is. Consider taping your own eulogy and broadcasting to large screen TVs set up around the grounds at your services! If you've got the money, you may even consider airing it as an infomercial.

Be sure to shoot yourself with side lighting (for dramatic effect) and (if your budget permits) to include some snappy graphics like TV news does when a war breaks out. Maybe even arrange to edit in some of your own news footage and home movies to break the tape up! Don't forget to put credits at the end, and, to keep everyone's attention, to roll your eyes up into your head a few times, yell out at your guests, make scary ooooooh-type sounds, etc. You can even tell a few good jokes to loosen up the crowd. Remember, you're the star of this production!

Your guests will want to move on to the hors d'oeuvres and cocktails ASAP so make your tape a real grabber.

VHS copies also make great commemorative souvenirs.

Script your eulogy videotape carefully before you begin recording. This is not the place for ad-libbing. The better your tape, the more you'll sell.

The Layman's Guide to Suicide

Here are some one-liners to weave into your video script . . .

- I've got my own show!
- Hey Aunt Florence . . . drop that shrimp!
- Stay tuned . . . there's much more to come . . .
- Luckily, I captured my last few minutes on tape, so here it is in slow motion.
- By the way, did you ever hear the one about . . .
- If you wish to purchase a VHS copy of this tape for home viewing, get a pen or pencil to copy down the number that I'll be flashing on the screen.
- The bar has been set up atop my casket, and this time the drinks really are on me!
- Here's my watch. It took a lickin' but it kept on tickin'.
- And now for a very important announcement from your sponsor . . .
- We're experiencing technical difficulties, please stand by.
- Live! From my services, it's me!
- Who wants to sing a song? C'mon now, everyone join in . . . "99 cans of beer on the wall, 99 cans of beer . . ."

As you're making your tape, remember that timing is everything. For instance, if you time it right, you could be yelling, "Hey! Quit shoveling that dirt on me," or "I can't breathe, let me outta here!" just as you're being dropped in. And, of course, as guests are departing the cemetery, you should be waving goodbye and saying, "Thanks for coming."

If you do this eulogy tape right, it may even be picked up as a miniseries!

The Layman's Guide to Suicide

Techniques

A Selection of Foolproof Techniques to Satisfy the Most Discriminating of Tastes

DO *NOT* TRY ANY OF THESE TECHNIQUES. The techniques described are extremely dangerous and will result in severe bodily injury or, better yet, death.

Well, it appears that you're already bound and determined to pull the plug. The fact is, it's probably easier to kill yourself than to stay alive, so there's no need to dwell on technique. And, more than likely, you're a little confused and distraught as you read this. Don't despair. There are thousands of ways to meet with success in your endeavor. Surely the big question in your mind is which method is best for me? As you must realize, there are many ways to succeed, and each has its own features and benefits.

On the following pages you will find but a few of the thousands of possible techniques. Each is custom-tailored to make your upcoming demise a piece of cake and, in some cases, a spectacular event for onlookers as well.

The Layman's Guide to Suicide

Key To The Ratings

Spectator Value

- 🪦🪦🪦🪦🪦 Grandstands Required
- 🪦🪦🪦🪦 Heavy Rubber-necking/ Curiosity Seekers
- 🪦🪦🪦 Stops Passers By/ BBQ Activity
- 🪦🪦 Rescue Personnel/ Stray Dogs Only
- 🪦 No One

Media Coverage Potential

- 🪦🪦🪦🪦🪦 Feature Film Guaranteed
- 🪦🪦🪦🪦 Nat'l Networks/Wire Services
- 🪦🪦🪦 Made for TV Documentary
- 🪦🪦 Local Newspaper and Radio
- 🪦 Town Gossip/Local News

To make the choice easier, we've rated each technique in terms of potential media coverage and spectator value. If you're taking your life, you may desire a little fanfare or at least some attention. Five gravestones is best; one gravestone is worst. When reviewing the techniques, be sure to check the rating to determine which method is best for you.

When you consider technique, you have to determine what you want out of it . . . unusual methods are rewarded with greater coverage.

Study the ratings chart above to see what we mean. A technique rated "five gravestones" in the spectator value category means grandstands will be required. On the other hand, "two gravestones" in the same category means the only spectators you can expect are rescue personnel and stray dogs. Of course, there are other considerations such as corpse condition and burial method selected, but those should be more or less obvious.

The Layman's Guide to Suicide

Taking the Train

Spectator Value 🚪🚪🚪🚪🚪 **Media Coverage** 🚪🚪🚪🚪🚪

For years now, people have been meeting with trains for two good reasons: it's sensational, and it's a real treat for spectators.

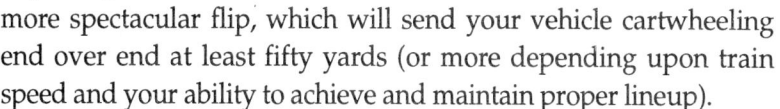

Trains are big heavy objects that, once rolling, take a long time to stop. Perfect!

First you need to select the right vehicle for your rendezvous. Refer to the consumer guide to find the subcompact that failed the government crash tests. Then, rather than simply accepting the common broadside, completely remove the tires and the front bumper, drive up and onto the tracks, and head directly toward the train (see illustration).

Although this maneuver requires greater skill, the result is a more spectacular flip, which will send your vehicle cartwheeling end over end at least fifty yards (or more depending upon train speed and your ability to achieve and maintain proper lineup).

Don't get yourself in a panic. Leave early and refer to a current train schedule for meeting times. To avoid being deafened by the sound of the train horn, roll up all of your windows.

And don't forget to buckle up . . . IT'S THE LAW!

TIP—Don't wait on the tracks . . . it's dangerous!

The Layman's Guide to Suicide

So Simple It's Automatic!

Spectator Value 🪦🪦　　　　　　**Media Coverage** 🪦🪦🪦

This trip begins and ends in your own auto garage (or that of a friend or loved one). A method that's tailor-made for the homebody and the car buff, it requires only your car and ordinary household items.

Before you embark on your journey, stop at the local convenience store. Be sure to use the rest room and fuel up with high octane LEADED fuel (a half tank will do). Then pack those essential things that will make your trip more comfortable. Some snacks, your favorite cassettes, your pets (to stay awake), a one-half mile length of ordinary clothes dryer exhaust hose, and a pair of handcuffs (without the key) will do fine. Before you get too excited, don't forget to grab the dryer exhaust hose and run it up from your auto exhaust to the interior of your vehicle. Then, jump in. It won't be necessary to buckle your seat belt, but do remember to roll up the windows. Clip the handcuffs from your wrist to the steering wheel, crank up the stereo, set the air conditioner to recirculate, sit back and relax.

TIP—Carports and open fields may take longer.

The Layman's Guide to Suicide

Cooking with Gas

Spectator Value   **Media Coverage**

People have been sticking their heads in ovens ever since the advent of natural gas. Although the fumes alone can kill, if you've got gas and if you can strike a match, you've got a winning combination. Even if you don't cook, you will.

To get started, shut, tape, and seal all the windows and doors in your kitchen. Preheat your oven as you would to broil a steak, but snuff out the pilot light and leave the door open. And don't forget to turn on all stove burners to high.

FOR SAFETY MAKE SURE NO OPEN FLAMES ARE PRESENT.

Leave the kitchen, tell your neighbors that there's a gas leak and they should evacuate the area, wait 30 minutes (to allow them to gather their belongings), and then return.

Pull up a stool and, wearing goggles, a swim mask, or dark glasses (to avoid eye injury), peer directly into the oven. Then, without hesitation, pull out your favorite matchbook.

TIP—Don't breathe the fumes because they can be hazardous.

The Layman's Guide to Suicide

The High Speed Crash with a Twist

Spectator Value **Media Coverage**

Many folks choose the high-speed vehicular crash as a means to the end and rightfully so. Already the traditional is a high-visibility method, but add a few props and extensive media coverage is all but guaranteed. (In fact, you may even preempt regular programming.)

Crashing into a solid stationary object (like a bridge abutment) ensures that your vehicle will end up safely off the road and that motorists will get a good look at you without stopping traffic altogether. NO MATTER HOW CAUTIOUS YOU ARE, EXPECT EXTENSIVE RUBBERNECKING.

The trick is to load your backseat with cement blocks (stack 'em high) and round up a few of the neighborhood pets to bring along. DON'T BUCKLE UP. Take position three-quarters of a mile downrange, grit your teeth (optional), and accelerate briskly. To avoid distraction, keep the pets in the back. When you are within twenty feet of the abutment, CUT OVER. Even though you may be anxious, don't jump the gun! Grass and uneven pavement can slow you down, or worse, cause you to lose control of your vehicle!

If impact is made at the proper speed, your compact vehicle should be transformed into a subcompact. The cement blocks will aid in reducing the bodies of the pets (as well as yours) to pulp. A field day for the paramedics, you'll easily baffle the rookies as they sift through the wreckage! In addition, your vehicle will be easily transportable by crane, thus alleviating traditional towing charges. If done correctly, a casket will not be required. A great time and money saver, eliminating embalming, viewing, and essentially all burial costs outside of digging the hole and dropping you and your car in.

TIP—When selecting your bridge abutment, make sure not to choose a radar trap since the flashing lights of a police car behind may distract you, hampering your ability to concentrate on your target.

The Layman's Guide to Suicide

Take Lightning into Your Own Hands

Spectator Value   **Media Coverage**

Here's one for the nature lover, and it's a real crowd pleaser! We all know lightning is powerful stuff, and a single targeted bolt of lightning makes high tension wires seem like static electricity.

Lightning always strikes the tallest object, which makes radio transmitting towers ideal (but a sturdy aluminum ladder set up on wet ground in a open field will do in a pinch). For this example, we'll assume you can find a tower.

Be sure to pack a lunch, your raincoat, a stopwatch, plenty of tinfoil, and your ALUMINUM umbrella. Aluminum is a fabulous conductor, and an open umbrella will keep you dry as well.

Ascend the transmitter tower right before the storm approaches (the tingle you may feel is just the signal, don't worry). As you clutch the top, with the red beacon flashing in your face, secure yourself to the tower with your belt. Try to reach the top before it starts raining; otherwise the tower will be slippery and you could fall and injure yourself.

The Layman's Guide to Suicide

When you hear the first clap of thunder, grasp the aluminum shaft of the umbrella (NOT THE PLASTIC HANDLE) in your right hand and, in your left, grip a section of the tower. YOU BECOME THE CONNECTION BETWEEN BOLT AND TOWER. Don't forget to wrap the tinfoil around your forearms securely.

With your stopwatch, time the difference between the thunder and the lightning. At about the one-second mark, you should be there. Pay no mind to the crowd on the ground. Just yell back that you can't hear them yelling, "JUMP!" If by some unfortunate chance the storm passes you by, simple—just do a swan dive.

TIP—Bring along weenies or marshmallows and a cellular phone (to talk to the press while you're waiting).

Quickies for the Poor

Not everyone can afford an elaborate suicide, so here are some methods for the budget conscious.

Jay Walking
(Your name doesn't have to be Jay.)

Spectator Value   **Media Coverage**

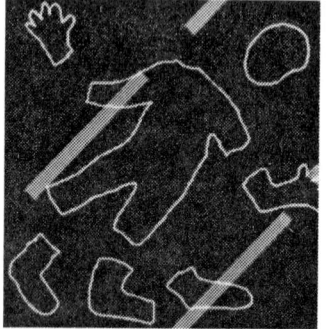

Plenty of people skip out in front of traffic every year, but few consider diving into it. The first step is to locate a freeway overpass by checking the traffic report to see which freeways are flowing smoothly (high-speed, bumper-to-bumper traffic works best). WEAR A HELMET TO AVOID HEAD INJURY. Your carcass will likely spread into all three lanes (see illustration), so perish the thought of an open casket but do consider numbering your arms and legs for the rescue squad.

For the Mountain Bike Enthusiast

Spectator Value **Media Coverage**

Like to bike? Even if you don't have one, picking up a nice

mountain bike is a snap, and you certainly need not worry about the consequences of its being reported stolen. Starting at the top of a steep, winding canyon road, snip the brake cable and hop on. Take a hard left or right anywhere you see fit. If you're not comfortable on two wheels, strap into a wheelchair, same technique.

Freeway Skateboarding

Spectator Value 🪦🪦🪦   **Media Coverage** 🪦🪦🪦🪦

Here's a new one for the adventurous that we haven't seen yet. Wearing a wet suit and knee and elbow protection, hop on your skateboard and hide behind a toll booth with a rope securely fastened around your waist. At the other end of the rope, tie a lasso. Wait for a car to pass with a trailer hitch, muckle a hold of it, hold on tight and squat (to avoid being seen by the driver). At about 63 mph (or before you lose control), SKATE LEFT.

Can't Afford a Car, but Got a Motorcycle?

Spectator Value 🪦   **Media Coverage** 🪦

For motorcycle enthusiasts, one taut piano wire strung between trees across your favorite stretch of highway at neck level works just like a cheese slicer. Any questions?

The Layman's Guide to Suicide

Razor Blades
(and Other Sharp Household Objects)

Spectator Value 🪦   **Media Coverage** 🪦

Anyone can slit his or her wrists so we won't even discuss it here, but have you ever thought about sticking your whole arm in a wood chipper? A blender? A chain saw? A garbage disposal? Through a plate glass window? Blades are dull... and most of you wimps will pass out after the first slash! If you feel compelled, cut out the blade printed here and practice first.

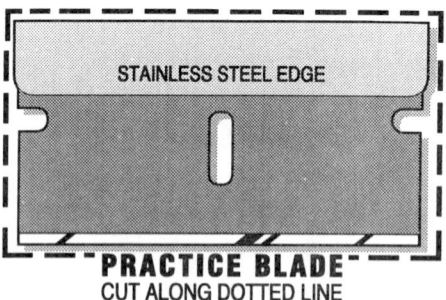

Nearing Hunting Season, Deer?

Spectator Value 🪦   **Media Coverage** 🪦

Wearing earth tones, wave antlers overhead and dart from tree to tree; or skip the antlers, tape a target to your chest, and pop up at your local rifle range.

The Layman's Guide to Suicide

Cooking for Pacemaker Patients

Spectator Value 🎭🎭🎭🎭🎭   **Media Coverage** 🎭🎭🎭🎭🎭

Pacemakers and microwaves don't mix, and that's the good news! With an older one, you can cook your food and yourself at the same time!

The proper tools are a must. Small units don't do the job. However, an older, leak-prone, commercial 1,500-watt unit will work fine.

Since it makes little sense to buy your own unit for one-time use, seek an outside source that has a unit meeting these specs. Restaurants and convenience stores tend to be prepared for those of you seeking a charitable situation.

Many convenience stores are open 24 hours (isn't that convenient?), and most are within walking distance of your home.

When you reach the location of your choice, don't dawdle. Select a favorite microwavable food, walk up to the machine smartly and without hesitation. Avoid popcorn. If there's a line, make small talk. Now's the time to celebrate by proposing a toast to yourself before your pacemaker begins to skip like an old record. When it's your turn, place your food inside, and quickly hug the machine like a dear friend. Using setting number 5, press start, clutch, and dive. If executed properly, you'll be done long before the timer goes off. CAUTION: NEVER USE THE DEFROST MODE.

TIP—Place only one item at a time in the microwave to avoid undercooking.

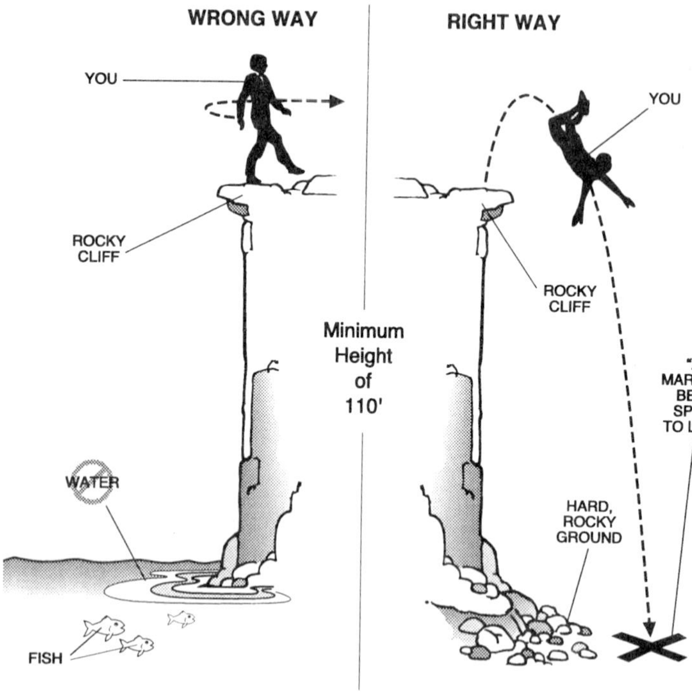

The Layman's Guide to Suicide

WRONG WAY — YOU, ROCKY CLIFF, Minimum Height of 110', WATER, FISH

RIGHT WAY — YOU, ROCKY CLIFF, HARD, ROCKY GROUND, "X" MARKING BEST SPOT TO LAND

Dry Land Cliff Diving

Spectator Value   **Media Coverage**

Here's one for true diving enthusiasts, rugged outdoorsmen, thrill seekers, nature lovers, and the like.

Mark an X at the spot in which you intend to land on the ground. Then climb to the top of your favorite cliff. Running starts are optional, but NEVER JUMP WHEN THE TIDE IS IN. To meet with success, timing is everything! Since it will be your last dive of the day, be adventurous. Try that triple-twist, one-and-a-half pike you never thought you could master, or go for the ultimate swan dive.

TIP—Watch out for rocks, crustaceans, and small boats.

The Layman's Guide to Suicide

Jumpin' for Joy
(or Anyone Else You Can Blame)

Spectator Value 🪦   **Media Coverage** 🪦🪦

Anyone can jump off a bridge, but what if you were to land the wrong way? Don't chance it. Ensure success with a tall bridge and a bungee cord just slightly longer than the bridge height. The advantage here is that, rather than bouncing once or twice, you're assured of at least six or seven bounces. Refer to the chart below.

BRIDGE HEIGHT	100'	200'	300'	400'	500'	600'	700'	800'
BUNGEE CORD LENGTH	110'	210'	310'	410'	510'	610'	710'	810'

Tornado Chasing
(Going with the Wind)

Spectator Value 🪦   **Media Coverage** 🪦🪦

Well, you can click your heels with this one 'til you're blue in the face and you still won't come back. Kansas and Florida have the most, so move there first, preferably into a mobile home. It's simple. When you see one, drive right into it. If it comes to your backyard, strap yourself to an old desk, hide under a picnic table, or stand spread-eagle and weather the storm, bucko. Dress for windy conditions and watch out for flying objects. Be sure to toss the weather map and hang on tight to your suicide note.

Happy landings!

Tub Toast

Break out the bubbly! This will be one of the hottest baths you've ever had. You'll toast yourself with a nice, relaxing warm bath and your 1,500-watt hair dryer.

First, draw the water in the tub, step in, and relax. Plug in your hair dryer and turn it on to HIGH. Make sure your hands are dry. Next either drop the dryer in directly, or try your luck at juggling. Either way, once it hits the water, it will make more than a splash and voilà! You're toast. If you're in a pinch and don't own a hair dryer, a four-slice toaster will work just as well.

CAUTION—Tub water will heat up rapidly once the dryer is dropped in.

The Layman's Guide to Suicide

Making Your Arrangements

With proper planning, you'll get just what you want in the end.

Although you'll likely be bubbling over with excitement as you make your first call to the funeral parlor, try to stay calm and keep your wits about you. In discussing your pre-need arrangements, the trick is not to let on how soon your need will be! And don't be discouraged if the consultant is not as excited and upbeat as you are.

There are four basic disposal methods to consider: traditional in-ground burial, aboveground burial, cremation, and burial at sea.

When considering how you wish to have your body handled, keep in mind that the suicide technique you choose and the resulting condition of your remains may eliminate the need (or possibility) of some of the extras, such as a viewing, a casket, or even a funeral, so don't let them talk you into extras you won't need.

A Wake or Not?

Your wake will be the last time your friends, relatives, and loved ones will have an opportunity to get together with you, so try to show everyone a good time. Consider taking your wake out of the home by renting a hall that can handle all of your entertainment and catering needs.

Skip the little sandwiches and plan exciting hors d'oeuvres that tie in with your own technique. Fried foods are obvious if your method left you in that condition, sushi or smorgasbord is appropriate if you fell apart, and red meat goes with just about anything you could have conjured up.

A good DJ can keep things going long into the night, and it's nice to throw in a few contests to get people mingling. If you're on a tight budget, you can charge for the food à la carte at the door by selling food tickets. Leave plenty of room for dancing and keep your casket, the food table, and cash bar at one end out of the way of traffic. Rely on hall staff to plan your wake with you; they're the professionals. Your wake can be just another blasé affair, or it can be the talk of the town!

Location, Location, Location!

Carefully consider where you want your grave site. To ensure frequent visitation, choose an appealing spot that will inspire family and friends to come and pay their respects often. A popular resort area or theme park is ideal. Pick a place you've been dying to go . . . such as Hawaii, the Caribbean, or even Europe!

Grave Markers, Headstones, and Tombs

Markers range from mammoth marble monuments to tiny plastic garden stakes. Your choice depends on your budget, personal tastes, and how prominently you wish to stand out in the cemetery.

If you're shy and wish to blend in with the crowd, go with the little unobtrusive plastic stake (beware that the lawn mower chews these up). If you're an extrovert, go with the largest monument zoning will allow (preferably something that can be seen from the air). And if you want a place where visitors can get in out of the rain (or even spend the night) look into a tomb. Also neon is available is some areas, but check signage restrictions.

The Ride to the Cemetery

Although you could settle for having your casket transported in a friend's station wagon, pickup truck, or boat trailer, why not organize a real Hollywood procession? With enough vehicles and motorcycle cops in the motorcade you can make it look just like the president's in town! It won't be cheap, but you can recoup some of the limo rental costs by charging $5.00 each for the ride (everyone wants a ride in a limo!), plus $3.50 for cocktails en route. For the kids, a $2.00 hayride to the cemetery is an unexpected treat! To generate more cash, sell ad space on the sides of the limos (magnetic signs or banners). With a little incentive (like a keg of beer at the end of the ride), you can probably get the whole town to join in behind with their lights on! Make a small donation to the fire department and perhaps you can add a hook and ladder in as well. Consider a charter bus if you're expecting a big crowd (to avoid parking problems), and be sure to contact the media early enough for them to get the copter up for aerial coverage of the event.

The Layman's Guide to Suicide

Grave Site Decorations and Souvenirs

Remember, you wanted to take your own life, so what's there to grieve about? This is a festive occasion so decorate! Once your plot is excavated, be sure to arrange for plenty of streamers, banners, balloons, even Grand Opening flags! These commemorative souvenirs can be personalized with your name and the date of your birth and death and sold to offset the cost of your service. After they drop you in, allow guests to pitch in with their own souvenir shovels!

Have generators and lights on hand just in case the event runs past dusk, and don't forget to cordon off an area for the camera crews and to keep out weirdo cult groups and necrophiliacs! If rain is in the forecast, have a tent available as well.

Music Sets the Mood and More . . .

Music at the wake and the funeral is essential to drown out the voices of the feuding relatives. Subliminal messages can be added to subtly remind your loved ones of how much they will truly miss you or how much they are to blame, or even to advertise your friends' businesses. You might even consider selling your funeral's soundtrack on cassette or CD.

If You Fail . . .
. . . *And can still read this.*

It is unthinkable, but what if? A sequel offering more methods is in the works, but much depends on if you are still able to read, walk, or move. Actually much depends on if you are still able to get to the bookstore, period.

If you are still determined (and now possibly more than ever), go back, reread. You should have taken notes. What happened anyway? Chickened out halfway? Did you follow the instructions carefully, or did you think you could wing it on your own?

If you did fail, first and foremost, find your suicide note and destroy it immediately! By doing so, at least you'll be able to plan your next attempt from home!

Also, take inventory of your body parts and their remaining functionality. Depending on your current condition, you may not have all the options available (in terms of technique) that you had the first time around.

The Layman's Guide to Suicide

The Obituary

You don't need to settle for run-of-the-mill if you write your own.

Even if you choose the basics, make sure your obituary reads the way you want it to by taking the time to write it yourself!

Make the most of it by taking some poetic license. Draw sympathy, add drama to your life story, describe your technique, talk about why you're not in the "Living Well" section, and lay blame on those you hate.

You can even make your passing sound like it was a greater loss than it was by listing your own bogus accomplishments and milestones (editors never check these things). Plus, if you plan on raising funds at the gate, you can promote your services by listing time, place, and a brief description of the ceremony.

This is your last chance to pump yourself up and the best way to advertise to the public, so go for it!

The Layman's Guide to Suicide

Obituaries

John Doe—passed away at 6:20 P.M., May 15, 1997. Unknown to many, he was considered to be one of the country's top physicists, highly instrumental in the first Apollo mission as well as in the development of the first nuclear submarine. He will be remembered as the unhappy father of three awful children and husband of a tyrannical wife. His charred body was found welded to the top of radio station WXYZ's transmitter tower. He was holding the frame of an aluminum umbrella in one hand and had his arms and legs wrapped in tinfoil. Lightning was clearly the cause of death. No casket was required. The wake will include an elegant buffet, live musical entertainment, the world's largest champagne fountain, imported truffles, and ice sculptures in the shape of a lightning bolt and a transmitting tower. The wake is scheduled to begin promptly at 8:00 P.M. on Thursday May 22; the funeral is scheduled for May 25 at Preston's Memorial Gardens. Dress is semiformal, and admission is free to both events.

Jane Doe—passed away at 7:00 P.M. on May 15, 1997. Throughout her career, Ms. Doe was listed in various publications as one of the world's ten most desirable women. Her vehicle struck a bridge abutment at high speed on I-10 near Castleberry. The vehicle hit the abutment with such force as to reduce it to a two-foot by two-foot cube (approximately). In addition (and to this date unexplained), numerous pets and cement blocks were found in the vehicle along with Ms. Doe. A viewing is not scheduled; however, a Black Tie Gala Fund-Raising Event and Funeral is planned for Thursday May 28 at Memorial Gardens from 3:00 P.M. to 9:00 P.M. All arrangements for the fund-raiser were made and paid for by Ms. Doe in advance. At 6:30 P.M. Ms. Doe will be buried in her vehicle by crane. A $5.00 donation at the gate is requested by Ms. Doe to cover damage her vehicle caused to the bridge abutment. For directions and more information, please call 1-900-NEW-ABUT. The cost of the call is $2.95 with proceeds going directly to the Department of Highways. The public is invited.

The Layman's Guide to Suicide

Terminology

Classic Ways to Say "I'm Dead"

- Kicked the bucket
- Bought the farm
- Pulled the plug
- Shut off the lights
- Took the big step
- Bit the dust
- Dropped dead
- Kicked off
- Departed
- Met my maker
- Passed away
- Passed on
- Died
- Flat-lined
- Stopped ticking
- Took the gas pipe
- Bit it
- Went to the big ___ in the sky

Elegant Ways to Say "Good-Bye"

- Hasta Luego
- Sayonara
- Au Revoir
- Ciao
- Arrivederci
- Later

Things to Yell While You're Doing It

- Holy shit!
- Owwwww!
- Whoa!
- Yippeeeee!
- Gnarly, dude!
- Over and out!
- Watch out below!
- I'm outta here!
- Cowabunga!
- Wheeeeeeeeeeeeeeeeeeeeeee!
- Help me!
- Uh-oh!
- Oh boy!
- Geronimo!
- Oh my god!
- This is gonna hurt!

Taking Others with You
Is it really more fun to go with more than one?

You're contemplating suicide, and you say to yourself, "Hey, maybe instead of just killing myself, I could take out a whole group of innocent people or show that special someone how much his/her misdeed meant to me, by snuffing out his/her life as well." Not good thinking.

If you take loved ones with you, they won't get to experience the lifelong guilt you desire. And, by taking a group, although you could provide them with the opportunity to experience the wonders of modern medicine and offer their families a wealth of last-minute plans and activities, it is simply not a good idea.

If you're really stuck on bringing a guest along when you go, find someone with similar interests and goals. You might volunteer as a counselor on a suicide hotline . . . or call one for referrals. Or seek out qualified individuals in state mental hospitals.

Although you may feel that society as a whole is the cause of your demise, you can't take the entire world with you (unless you're the leader of a superpower). So cool out. Taking the lives of innocent people is not only selfish, it's idiotic. Even though you may be a complete and total failure, you don't want to be labeled an idiot on top of that. If you are really stuck on bringing others along, blow-up dolls, gerbils, or a neighbors' pet will do.

The Layman's Guide to Suicide

Parting Words to Live By

Bet you didn't realize what a hassle it is to kill yourself, did ya?

Now that you see how much goes into suicide, maybe it's time to give life a second thought. Life ain't no bowl of cherries all the time, but as compared to the unknowns and variables of the afterlife, it seems to be the safer bet.

Regardless of your predicament, you can see from this book that killing yourself is going to be one big pain-in-the-ass (or other vital body part), and it's going to be a real downer for everyone.

Notes: